T0193415

WHAT NIGHTFALL HOLDS

RICHARD SLOANE

authorHOUSE®

AuthorHouse™
1663 Liberty Drive
Bloomington, IN 47403
www.authorhouse.com
Phone: 1 (800) 839-8640

Published by AuthorHouse 08/21/2019

ISBN: 978-1-7283-2411-1 (sc)
ISBN: 978-1-7283-2410-4 (e)

Print information available on the last page.

This book is printed on acid-free paper.

EVEN IN THE FACE OF HEARTACHE

★ ★ ★

Ever since you gave me life I have only caused you pain;

here we are, three decades later, and still you don't complain.

You've come to visitation and bonded me out of jail,

yet even amidst all my crap, I know your love won't fail.

You epitomize loyalty, with never a question asked,

and if ever I need some help, you come running fast.

I have often wondered why I've never heard you whine;

in regards to all my flaws, you surely must be blind.

My wondrous memories of you are far too many to count;

your love cannot be measured, of that I have no doubt.

When we are reunited your lips will erupt with smiles;

your beauty is inspiring and your grins will stretch for miles.

I know that I have hurt you with my numerous crimes,

yet your morals can't be broken, even in difficult times.

Your character is like a mountain with an unreachable crest;

when compared to other mothers you always emerge the best.

There is no way to show my thanks for all that you have done,

for in the lottery that awards us mothers, I have clearly won.

It's no miracle that your radiance is dwarfed by all your love;

I'll forever extol your virtues, because they fit you like a glove.

There are none that can dethrone you or ever take your place;

you can topple governments with a mere glimpse of your face.

I swear I'll do my best to atone for my misdeeds,

but as long as you're my mother, you're all our family needs.

INSIDE MAN

*   *   *

Slipping and splashing, fleeing through the rain,
I am just a pawn in some twisted game.

Stumbling and tripping, in woods so dark and cold,
fright urges me on from a creature impossibly old.

Worrying and frantic, near an emotional overdose, my ears
detect a noise from something unnaturally close.

Running and dashing, I look behind, but nothing there;
a formless beast awaits, and I know not where.

Gasping and panting, I cannot catch my breath; these
weary lungs are a sign of my impending death.

Screaming and despondent, with my throat raw and sore,
I cry out for help where there is none in store.

Terrified and unaware, legs burning with no rest, how
long can I continue without salvation manifest?

Quivering and freezing, with my energy depleted, up
ahead, sanctuary is spied, a lodge I imagine heated.

Oblivious and ignorant, now my safety seems assured, yet,
tireless even in my sprint, this monster has endured.

Powerful and patient, the beast grows ever near, but it lives only in our minds as the embodiment of fear.

Coaxing and convincing, our logic it tries to steal, by impressing in our minds a view that isn't real.

Suddenly and clearly, my sanity is renewed; from what was I running or trying to elude?

Discerning and perceiving, the fuel that fed the beast, was merely insecurity, on which my fear could feast.

Undeterred and resolute, I won't run any longer, nor hide from any phobia, for I am now far stronger.

THE SPECTRUM

★　　★　　★

My shredded heart, the muscle dead; lips are blue and limpness spread.

The flowing tears, the wracking heaves pound
upon me with armored greaves.

Years will pass and seasons change; the outside world becomes so strange.

This deep abyss, a prison cell; the ebon void's end, no one can tell.

Calendars are replaced, gray hair sprouts; old
friends forget, tension mounts.

Must I concede and resign myself to placing my life upon a shelf?

Yet memories emerge; my happiness recalled,
of long ago before progress stalled.

Sadness wasn't real, heartache was naught; there
was no need for such things to be fought.

Surrounded by love, my youth as a boy, was
bolstered by friends who knew only joy.

Reminded of this, my purpose renewed; I'll
overcome my own inner feud.

Otherwise I'm doomed, because death lingers close
and failure is that which I fear most.

But I can recover, I will survive and regain my life, for which I'll strive.

STREWN

★   ★   ★

Broken promises, broken dreams, pieces scattered all around.

A broken kingdom for broken kings; his
weeping queen holds a broken crown.

Broken souls, broken minds, tears filling a broken glass.

A broken road just bends and winds to a
broken future, from a broken past.

Broken bonds and broken trust shatter faith that cannot mend.

A broken locket lies covered in dust, with no neck on which to suspend.

Broken down with broken bones under a
broken cross on a mound of stones.

Broken sobs, broken moans; this broken life ever onward drones.

Broken kids from a broken home and parents with broken hearts,

these all gave birth to a broken poem that
describe a man with broken parts.

WARNING

★　　★　　★

For millennia innumerable were known the merits of deceit;
our species learned to mislead before we could even speak.

As children test their parents with joke on top of scheme,
we see falsehood easily adopted as the majority theme.

People lie every day as a normal mode of defense; it has
become second nature to dress up in pretense.

Never has perfection been something I could claim,
nor have I stepped on others in my race to fame.

Some people though are skilled, appearing honest and loyal,
but when they try to play me, it sets my blood to boil.

The lack of all things genuine has made me very cynical;
authenticity is so scarce that many think it's mystical.

Don't take me to be gullible or swayed by any excuse; this
brings about the liar's doom, which I'll happily induce.

I raise awareness of this deception by waxing lyrical, though
nothing can rid our world of lies, short of a miracle.

Integrity is a missing trait common to the inferior, and
those who don't possess it will rot in hell's interior.

My words must spur these traitors to hastily retreat; they should
avoid me at all costs, lest their campaign taste defeat.

Instead of targeting me in some ploy, I'd best be left alone, or
the backlash of such ignorance will be very widely known.

Women like to use lust as a cover for their guile; in my
youth it was effective, but has since become futile.

Leave all trickery at the door and we can get along fine, unless
some schooling is in order, for I can gladly broadcast mine.

CAN YOU?

★   ★   ★

Can you hear me scream when it is only in my mind?

If I try to speak, will I have a voice to find?

Do you feel my rage when I'm at the end of my rope?

Will I be committed when I can no longer cope?

Can you even see me or am I invisible?

Could it be paranoia or is it hardly sensible?

It's hard to tell the difference when I am so confused,

the busy streets and busy lives around leave me bemused.

Can you feel my pain when I am torn apart?

Or do you just ignore me because you have no heart?

Can you stop the chaos that you yourself create?

Or will you just continue to keep me in this state?

Can you start pretending to even find a way?

Because alone I fear it is a price I can no longer pay.

HORIZON'S INTENT

*   *   *

Black clouds are roiling and slowly growing near;

thunder roars hard, and in many, instills fear.

A monster storm approaches that will surely be quite rough,

yet all the prepping you have done is nowhere near enough.

You can't begin to fathom the ferocity heading your way,

and in light of your stupidity, you decide to stay.

Now this destructive force is unlike any other,

though if you manage to survive, your body will forever shudder.

Terrible fury such as this leaves no structure on the ground;

you'd better say a prayer that your body will be found.

Splinters will be all that remain of what you used to own;

even your neighbors won't recognize where you built your home.

Weather radar is at a loss in identifying this storm;

it seems to have a mind of its own, rapidly changing form.

Is this merely wind and rain, or is it something far worse?

Too bad you won't find out before you're loaded in a hearse.

These disasters rain down death on those caught in its path;

in its wake is only ruin and the residue of its wrath.

There is always one who thinks lightning can't strike him,

but in trying to avoid these bolts, his fate becomes too grim.

Such havoc described herein cannot ever be foreseen;

only the Almighty has the power to intervene.

The imminent signs, though plain to see, you opted to dismiss,

so give thanks to your ego and pride for sending you to the abyss.

RELIEF FOR THE ASKING

★   ★   ★

Confess to me, your faults and your fears, and
be not ashamed if you shed any tears.

Lay open to me your flaws and your burden, to
keep them inside will only leave hurting.

No matter the time, it's never too late. to rid
yourself this emotional weight.

There is no need to suffer for years, the shame
and regret your heart only bears.

Don't wait to get it off your chest, or else your mind will get no rest.

Although you feel guilty, your spirit heavy with pain,
your soul isn't filthy, but needs reborn again.

A tainted spirit is no one's fate, to be held down by fear.

Be renewed and rid of all hate, of those you hold so dear.

That grief and despair will keep you down, and
harm you like Christ's thorny crown.

Now take a deep breath and choose life over death;
this choice isn't one to be made in jest.

Everyone, even you, needs a friend, someone
to help you not break, but bend.

Confide in me and set yourself free, and
become the you that you wish to be.

REMORSELESS ENDEAVOR

★　　★　　★

Ask not how I cope with this blood on my hands,

nor ask of my rope, how many necks it demands.

Countless nights I've spent reaping as my righteous trade is plied;

I have no problem sleeping, for my actions are justified.

Rampant, run this planet's ghouls and the evil that they sire,

while violating unspoken rules that deem their future dire.

Someone must protect the meek from falling victim at crime scenes;

yet, I believe, against evil's freak, the ends vindicate my means.

No weapon is off limits or is any method banned

in my pursuit of vile dimwits, whom I plunder like a brigand.

They all deserve far worse than that which they inflict,

so their lives I forever curse, to punish by royal edict.

Not caring what their actions cause, only focused on the score,

why would they obey laws which they already ignore?

Many don't even bear traces of understanding or humanity;

smiles will adorn their faces where revulsion would surely be.

If ever given the slightest chance such dogs would mow us down;

were I weaker in my stance I'd merely sulk and frown.

But I can't stand still when no one else will act,

fiends that rape and kill must be stopped, that's a fact.

Who else will carry this mantle, should I choose to retire?

Could another, upon thugs trample, then garrote them with wire?

Determination, one must surely own before taking up this task,

and the skill to work alone, containing feelings behind a mask.

It is because of these reasons I've made this drastic choice;

Even throughout the changing seasons, I'll defend those without a voice.

BY THE LIGHT OF THE MOON

★   ★   ★

As dusk fills the sky my body starts to change,

and my senses extend beyond normal range.

When night draws close and shadows grow longer,

my yearning for night ops only grows stronger.

It's beyond my ability to give up this beef,

cause in this battle against evil I've been named chief.

As a lycan under moonlight sprouts fur and fang,

I don a harness from which weapons hang.

Some call me a phantasm, a demon or a ghoul,

but to the perpetrator, you're only a fool.

For I've made it my business to hunt you and yours,

and before my work is done you'll beg on all fours.

Using blade and baton, my fury rains hard;

basically, you've hoisted yourself on your own petard.

With my eagle eyes and the nose of a hound,

you leave too many clues that are easily found.

I'll spend all night closing in for the kill,

from which I derive a gratifying thrill.

No other rush can even begin to compare

to imparting upon scum such a lethal dose.

The dose I speak of is a midnight cocktail,

of both steel and lead that I can send by airmail.

But with bullets or fists, the job will be done

and you'll have bled out before the rising sun.

THE STRUGGLE FOR REDEMPTION

★　　★　　★

Restless is what I've always been, never caring for another.

Meant for me, my punishment bestowed upon my sister and brother.

Regret and remorse are the burdens I bear since I've realized my mistake.

Now I know what it's like to care in the midst of such heartache.

Years pass and I'm still behind steel while my family pays the price.

They got the raw end of the deal and my apology won't suffice.

How can I make up for what I've done and repair what's been destroyed?

Will I ever be able to have some fun while
not being criminally employed?

Part of me wants to never go back to those I've subjected to pain

for fear that I won't get on track and their lives I'll forever stain.

What the future holds, I don't know but I will surely do my best

to strive to let my love show, that I can pass this test.

If I have to do it alone, that's fine, yet I don't think that's the case,

cause I know your love will always shine upon my smiling face.

THE GRUDGE

★   ★   ★

My home has always been the dark; it's these places I've left my mark.

It's these places where you fear you'll die that
keep you awake and terrified.

You're always hiding and never seeking, all the while I'm slowly creeping

up behind to sink my knife into your neck to end your life.

I walk alone, forever with a grudge that gives
me the right to be your judge.

I'm at your trial to see it through and find you guilty, I'll surely do.

No amount of blood can slake my thirst, so
your blood I'll spill won't be my first.

To kill and cut, stab and gut, are the methods I'll use after the hunt.

Don't try to run cause you won't get far; your
feeble attempts aren't even sub-par.

Your end is near and I won't say how, for my eyes
have seen you and I can't stop now.

BLOOD MONEY

★　　★　　★

I'm paid to rid the world of scum, paid with 55 gallon drums.

These drums are filled with evil's blood and I'll
spill so much the world will flood.

It's not a currency that I'll spend, but let's hope that I can start a trend

to take it upon oneself to fight before the scum blots out the light.

In darkness blood does not seem red, but be assured they will be dead.

For I stalk my prey in darkest night using methods
that fill your dreams with fright.

How could one not want this pleasure? I get satisfaction beyond measure,

by bleeding out the rancid scum, and letting them die cold and numb.

There are many snakes upon this earth, raping
and hurting for all they're worth;

but they bleed red, just like us all and I'll be there to make them fall.

OF MICE AND MEN

★　　★　　★

My panache and my wit hath both waxen great,
fed by the propagation of fools I hate.

They populate channels and YouTube fail blogs by
uploading videos of their cats and dogs.

"Come hold my beer and then watch this.", before
grinning and bathing in malt-laden piss

are the words and deeds of a fat redneck hick, that
he does on a dare while holding his stick.

With no tinge of shame or any common sense their
minds are the very definition of dense.

Yet they survive with a 3rd grade reading level, and
basking in idiocy they continue to revel.

I detest and despise that kind of chump, and I
do not follow the Twitter chief Trump.

Nor have I been hit with an arrow from cupid
to make me care for people so stupid.

God didn't make these people so dumb to smoke
an ounce of crack and then hunt a crumb.

It's by their choices they've made no headway, so
amongst their own kind is where they can stay.

I haven't time for the remedial uncouth who care
not for differences between lies and truth.

Let them wither and die in pointless thought,
and may all their efforts be for naught.

You must distance yourself from ducks of this type,
while denouncing such irrelevant hype.

Lest you be changed with the ease of its taint, and
become like those so fickle and faint.

Take heed of these words, caution, and warning, or
my verbal slaughter will leave you mourning.

Just because you're a dunce doesn't mean I'll
quit roasting you on my internet spit.

AMERICA THE BEAUTIFUL

★   ★   ★

American made, American slaves, this cell is what America gave.

An American monkey rides our back on display
riding us down to an American grave.

American trucks, American bucks, is all that is sought by American sluts.

Trump's words are like crap from an American butt.
A middle finger salute for an America shut.

American speed, American greed; on those things Americans feed.

Instead of the patriot Americans need, our
best Americans continue to bleed.

Americans crying, Americans dying, an American
dream we're no longer buying.

Keep your excuses, there's no use in trying, and
don't take our guns or lead will be flying.

America sells, America, hell! Liberty isn't just an American bell;

We gave it all up for an American cell; avarice is why America fell.

MORE

★　　★　　★

Shattered and broken, tattered and torn, pictures
and letters from a soul that is worn.

Scattered and cracked, pieces and shards, fragments
of life from a heart that is shorn.

They've been held together for so long by mere bits,
the time has come to stop taking hits.

You are more than these pieces that lie on the floor;
there's more to be seen, just open the door.

No approval is needed, no consent, no permission.
Do not listen to this talk of derision.

Pick yourself up and dust yourself off. Pay no
attention to those who may scoff.

Hopeless and faithless are what you used to be,
but that's no life to live, it's easy to see.

There's more to life than what you have known, there's
more to living than what you have shown.

There's more to your tears than sadness and joy,
more to your love, you're more than a toy.

Take more time to be happy, and leave more behind,
for more is the endless search of mankind.

WHAT CANARIES DO

★   ★   ★

Why can't people just seal their lips regarding
things they know nothing about?

Why must they gift the police with their tips by
snitching with an obnoxious shout?

That kind of thing was widely despised, we
would punish to the fullest extent.

Those bastards feeding info devised to see how my illicit cash is spent.

Now, too plentiful are the rats who'll put your name on a kite.

No matter how much we act as cats, hunting them throughout the night.

They won't ever take their own charge or
proudly tell the cops to get screwed,

but into your business they'll quickly barge to
ensure an investigation gets brewed.

Expect even worse, cause they'll tell that too,
if it means they can stay out of jail.

The events they inform on won't be few, nor will they lack in detail.

What happened to their integrity is lost on me,
yet I know of two traits that they keep.

They're concise when telling the fuzz what they
see and dream of snitching in their sleep.

So keep your dirt hidden fron the squealers, for
they'd love to send the cops your way.

Whether you be killers, thieves, or dealers,
you'll be told on without delay.

LONESOME

★   ★   ★

Aimlessly searching, for emotions to fill the blue,
was all the forlorn man knew how to do.

Unable to find purpose or any happiness, he
predicts his future mediocre, maybe less.

Not a leader or a follower, with an empty heart,
since birth, he's been a loner from the start.

Companionship and camaraderie are alien to him,
the touch of a woman, a momentary whim.

Acceptance by anyone has never been achieved, yet
at this social failure he is somehow relieved.

This man sees no point in enrolling at some club where
he'd have to mingle and member's elbows rub.

His anxiety only ebbs with others at arms length, but
that's just a weakness he imagines in his strength.

Most times, it seems almost too much to bear as he
seeks closure, hidden he knows not where.

Many walk past him not caring if he's warm; no
one offers a nod, or shelter from the storm.

With a face never smiled upon, and constantly ignored,
whatever hope he had is gone, never restored.

Wandering the land in pursuit of an unknown ideal,
loneliness erupts, making him stumble and reel.

Lost and distraught, with despair clouding his vision,
potent distrust of others gets him closer to perdition.

If only he wasn't stubborn and had a little faith, his
weakness wouldn't hound or haunt him like a wraith.

People do exist that'll help him in some way, while
not being judgmental or expecting any pay.

So the man must choose to change, or die alone, even
when difficulties on his path can't be known.

Though the journey may be rough, if he is ready, there
are those who will ensure his steps are steady.

CERCA TROVA

★   ★   ★

We were torn apart a half decade ago; since then
this has been just a one man show.

In no way could I ask you to wait years for me,
knowing you'd be happier if I set you free.

Why can't I get you out of my mind? For you,
I would leave all my past behind.

If only the judge hadn't sent me away, who
knows where we might be today?

I hated to hurt you, but I had to decide what was
better for you before I went back inside.

However, Gates said it best in "Find You Again"
when he promised that he'd find his friend.

I don't have time to waste on anyone else after
giving you that special piece of myself.

I've been gone so long, you could be anywhere,
but wherever that is, I'll find you there.

Before I left you my sad days were few, and I
knew your love was likewise true.

Back then, my flaws didn't faze you a bit, as
long as our bodies, together, could fit.

The same can be said of this oath to you, so
wherever you'll be, my arrival is due.

With pounds in the trunk and a gun on my hip,
not even that would cause you to trip.

Never questioning the risks of being on my team,
you'd only smile at me as if I were a dream.

Every day I thought of you, now I'm finally out; our
paths will soon cross, of that have no doubt.

Waiting with your arms open I do not expect, nor
any of your commitments, will I disrespect.

I can't go on without seeing you once more, to prove
that even now, your memories, I adore.

No obstacle will hinder or slow me in my hunt; any
opposition will be met with force too blunt.

I can't afford to leave these words left unsaid, "These
years without you, I'd have rather been dead".

DARKNESS, MY BELOVED

★　　　★　　　★

The darkness is my wondrous bride who envelopes me in her arms.

Her arrival is assured like the incoming tide
and I yearn for her ebony charms.

She loves me for eternity and never fails to bathe me in her glory.

From windless nights to stormy gales I strive to learn her story.

She has witnessed so much evil lurk beneath her blackened shroud.

It is my task to battle evil's work and I will make her proud.

My work is not the work of Satan who only wishes to deceive;

I fight for the good, lest evil awaken and cease the innocent's reprieve.

She bestows upon me a charcoal cloak that renders me sight unseen;

I can sweep over land as silent as smoke and hide from eyes quite keen.

There is no shortage of work to be done or of evil blood to shed;

She forever speeds my feet to run, to punish evil in its bed.

She provides for me throughout the night and cools me with her breath,

So I will never give up this fight until my righteous death.

UNDETECTABLE

★   ★   ★

Don't waste time searching the airwaves for a clue while
hoping to connect me to some hint, tinge, or hue.

You write programs to sift through data unknown, praying
that my face on your monitor will be shown.

This software you've written, and quite handy it is, with
encryption and binary coded by a competent whiz,

still cannot sniff out my elusive trail, before I
render your efforts useless and stale.

Do you enjoy being shackled to that super fast tower, so
that you may make lesser men whimper and cower?

Yet I am invisible to your electronic tools, for I
operate abroad where there are no rules.

The years of training and study you've done won't
prepare you when the hunt has begun

because you rely on your own algorithm's work to
point you where in the shadows I lurk.

You'll find no footage of me, nor the slightest trace
of anywhere I've been, no matter the place.

Highly skilled and certified, though you might be,
you'll never pose a fraction of danger to me.

Even with all your applications on hand, you
could be feared in your part of the land;

but where I exist, you'll be unable to find or
even discern with your narrow mind.

Go and scan databanks and command servers galore! I'll
still remain hidden while you pointlessly explore;

as your eyes grow strained with the tapping of
keys, I will continue to do as I please.

BREEZY

★　　　★　　　★

The leaves are fluttering high in the trees,
waving at me, moved by the breeze.

They twist and they turn, flying on air, reminding me of flags at the fair.

The wind is so fresh and cool on my face, and
for this moment I would not replace.

Colorful balloons and shiny pinwheels spin and float in a flurry I feel.

Smoke that is rising from a smoldering fire is
caught on a current, higher and higher.

Birds and butterflies soar and they flit around
in a beautiful show they emit.

As the wind becomes calm I already miss it and
yearn for the next time it comes to visit.

THE WALK

★ ★ ★

Marching along, in single file, trudging on, mile after mile.

One after another, the men are worn, because
they know what lies in store.

They must fight till the battle's won, and
only then will their job be done.

A little closer, now they are, but they have only come so far.

Urged on by their sense of duty, in the end there will be no booty.

For it's in a war they must engage, before they begin to turn this page.

The trek is long, the hills are steep, and all this way there's been no sleep.

The weaker of the men may fall before commencing the fight at all.

Pushing on through fatigue and pain the men slog on down the lane.

There's no turning back, no retreat; to do so would mean defeat.

The strongest fighters are drawing near while the enemy shakes in fear.

When the combat has subsided, still there'll be two sides divided.

HER INDESCRIBABLE IRONY

★   ★   ★

The scent of lotus blossoms float through the air

and rays of sunlight are dispersed in her hair.

Upon seeing her smile, my knees grow weak;

turning this world just a little less bleak,

only because I've discovered a love so rare.

Her kisses ignite a fire in my blood,

while all other lips are but worthless crud.

She riles my passion with the faintest touch,

and to pique my interest won't take much.

My need for her is akin to a flood.

To know she is sad fully breaks my heart,

yet to rectify this I'll immediately start.

My mission to hear her laugh again,

for that is the duty of all real men.

I yearn for the chance to do my part.

Her loyalty cannot be stifled or bound

nor can deceit inside her be found.

She harbors no grudge or any ill will

and constantly sates my wants to their fill.

These traits she maintains with nary a sound.

I'm reduced to tears in studying her motive

as she woos me with lit candles votive.

Defining in beauty, with honey-sweet skin

and morals that are anything but thin;

to her, I am forever devoted.

SOLDIERS OF FORTUNE

★　　★　　★

Most of the time, I work alone, but I have a few good friends.

Their deeds of valor are unknown, yet on them I can depend.

I will never speak aloud their names, but they know who they are.

These men do not delight in games unless it's marksmanship from afar.

Such men are soldiers, men at arms, who never fail to watch my back,

and amidst flying lead and buzzing alarms
they keep the mission on track.

These men are not drafted, they volunteer to join our courageous ranks;

they personify honor without fear, with the
balls to take on Abrams tanks.

The jobs we do will frighten others who get anxious and afraid,

but my cohorts are hardcore brothers that would fall on a live grenade.

Right after I call, they quickly arrive, eager to lend a hand;

and with a firm sense of purpose, they strive,
heading straight into enemy land.

They will die to get the mission done and would give their lives for me,

but if that's the price to ensure that we've won,
then they'll reign forever in memory.

THE FACADE

★   ★   ★

The girl hides her pain behind a great illusion and
no one can help her in her seclusion.

Her shame is concealed by the wall she built; she
can hardly breathe, overcome by the guilt.

Her life is in shambles and lying in ruins, nothing
helps, no matter what she is doing.

There once was a time she was happy and bright, but
it changed as quickly as day turns to night.

The light in her eyes has long since grown dim,
deeper in sadness when she thinks of him.

She hopes she can make it better someday, and
is willing to do whatever it takes.

One day soon the shine will restore and she
will be better than she was before.

If only she can hang on until that time, she will
learn what it feels like to be alive.

THE FEMALE DESCRIPTION

★   ★   ★

Treacherous women are worthless to me, liars
and connivers without loyalty.

The only one I've found that has any worth is the
one who was present at the time of my birth.

Other than her, all they do is complain, and
whine about money or their period pain.

Some men believe in honor amongst thieves, but a
cheater will burn you like a dry pile of leaves.

Scandalous women may hang out by shipyards, and
will play sailors like a cheap deck of cards.

Be on your guard against harlots and skanks or
you may get taken without even a thanks.

They'll hound you and drag you along through
the muck, all in the hope of a quick buck.

They'll throw you away with a flick of the wrist,
and from then on you'll never be missed.

I've learned firsthand that they aren't to be trusted,
unless by the cops you wish to be busted.

Please understand, I'm not dogging them all; there
are just so many on whom you can't call.

Not that I would, cause I handle my own; so I'm
riding solo and am fine being alone.

JUST A SIMPLE HOBBY

★   ★   ★

I love breaking in where I'm not supposed to be; local
authorities here like to call that burglary.

Pawn shop, jewelry store, or even a pharmacy; motion
sensors and cameras mean nothing to me.

Using lock picks, drills, and all kinds of tools, I make
the owners of these places look like fools.

Surveillance and subterfuge are part of my trade, as I
employ them over time a plan will be made.

I'm hunting guns, jewelry, and flat screen TV's; throw
some drugs in the mix and I'll make plenty cheese.

Not just anyone will be subject to this crime, as long
as you're insured you won't lose a dime.

I haunt the night loaded down with merchandise; many
places I have hit, but never more than twice.

Leaping fences and snapping jaws keep me in shape; I
can't afford to get sloppy; my freedom is at stake.

I leave no signs of my entry or any broken glass
as I heft a full duffel and exit with class.

Strutting with style, I carry off your wares; I mean,
your security is so lax, who even cares?

"Man, this bag of guns is heavy", I growl, as I make my way home from a night on the prowl.

Tomorrow when you survey the scene with a frown you can believe I'll be back on the town.

LIAR, LIAR

★　　　★　　　★

You twist the truth but don't call it a lie. You can't
have it both ways no matter how hard you try.

It has to be one way or the other. If you can't
accept that then why even bother?

I guess it must be hard to perceive from
someone who practices to deceive.

There are those who can see through your deceit and
will easily find your tales less than concrete.

You may think that you are witty and smart
but your level of lies is off the chart.

Your fiction and fables have become hollow,
hard to believe and harder to swallow.

There will be a time when your stories will crumble
and I can't wait to see the day that you stumble.

You've been getting away with deception too long
and it's time you begin to sing the truth song.

I'm sick and tired of making you think that I
believe all the lies, albeit they stink.

So this is the end of your fabrications or you
can look forward to your damnation.

THE NAMELESS NOMAD

★　　★　　★

As many years pass and boy becomes man, they
are slowly taught right from wrong.

Parents have jobs to do all that they can to guarantee
the lads grow up sure and strong.

But one boy's soul had a void inside where he
felt there was something amiss;

love wouldn't fill it and neither would pride, nor happiness, joy, or bliss.

This boy's mind was a real mystery to all who had dealings with him;

his search to find answers in man's history yielded
results that were too few and slim.

So he wandered the land, alone and withdrawn
and could not be satisfied,

until one morning at the break of dawn, in
the sun, his purpose was spied.

Amongst rays of light, a vision appeared, filtered through clouds and sky;

he witnessed his path, by his own choices
steered, forcing the wicked to die.

Fury and vengeance would fill up the hole
and with anger to fuel his heart,

he readied himself for his punishing role, eager to get a head start.

He does this to help others and find inner
peace, not for fortune and fame;

and if he has learned one thing at least, it's that not all of us are the same.

Night after night, with each finished task,
he grows more and more content;

now as a grown man, he is happy at last with
the way his life has been spent.

THE MAN

★ ★ ★

There was a man whose blood ran cold, for all
the lives that were bought and sold.

He came to decide one day that somehow he would make a way,

for those that had to pay the price, and for that his wrath would suffice.

He journeyed both far and near in search of
those who would come to fear.

The wicked ones, he came to learn, were the
ones he wanted most to burn.

He found them all and one by one, dealt them a hand played by his gun.

The captive ones were taken away and found their place anew to stay.

The man, now that his tasks were through, atoned
his sins through the men he slew.

EYES

★ ★ ★

Have you seen the eyes that stare?

They appear awake, yet unaware.

I'm sure you have seen these eyes,

full of hatred and full of lies.

Some have eyes full of life,

full of love, clear and bright.

Many have eyes dim and dull,

that's because they have no soul.

The beady eyes of evil men

show their wickedness within.

The precious eyes of a newborn child

know no sin and are reconciled.

CHANGES

★   ★   ★

She hasn't been happy in many a year, that she
will never be happy is her greatest fear.

A model is what she wanted to be, but in the mirror she can't bear to see.

Her lips are too thin, her hips are too wide, and
can't talk about how she feels inside.

She hates to see the lines on her face, and wishes there was a way to erase,

the ugly and tears, sorrow and fears, that keep her so sad, year after year.

The fact she doesn't have the power consumes her every waking hour.

To God above, she begs and pleads, to take her
away from this life that she leads.

Her loathing is all she thinks about, eating her up from the inside out.

All of the money and finer things cannot replace her shattered dreams.

NOWHERE ROAD

★   ★   ★

There's a lonely path that some may take,
that twists and turns like a snake.

This road leads far and near, through all the curves still goes nowhere.

Many travel down this course, and do so with no show of force.

Those who decide to take this trip must pay attention or lose their grip.

There are a few who trek this lane and reach the end not insane.

Some may follow and some may lead, and
some may find their hearts to bleed.

Those who reach the very last bend may be the ones to reach the end.

Through all the ups and downs they face,
there are but few who win the race.

WHAT WOULD I SAY?

★　　　★　　　★

If I saw you today after all these years would
I remain silent or voice my fears?

There are many things I want to say, but would I let you walk away?

Would I tell how you hurt me so or would I have to just let you go?

I ask my self, what would I say, if I saw you on the street today?

If I saw you today after all these years, would I be shedding happy tears?

I wonder if I could speak a word or if my voice could even be heard.

Would I feel free to express my love, or look for guidance from above?

I ask myself, what would I say, if I saw you on the street today?

What if you just passed me by without a glance or a reason why?

Would I scream and shout at you, or the
words come easily, out of the blue?

There are many things you should know, most of all how I need you so.

The question remains, what would I say, if I saw you on the street today?

ETERNITY

*   *   *

A remorseless face, full of disgrace, he wants
to hide what he's done in this place.

One thing, then another, he tries and he fails;
still he presses on, to no avail.

There is no way to hide from all, the things
that he's done, the lies are too tall.

His deeds have led him to purgatory, searching
for elusive fame and glory.

There is no way to escape from this hell, the lives
that he's taken, the souls that he fell.

This hell that only exists in his mind keeps
him from relief that he'll never find.

The regret and the torment, day after day, have
taken their toll, yet he must stay.

A shell of the man that he used to be, there is no way out that he can see.

His mind is shattered to the core, and here he remains, forevermore.

SOMETHING TO SEE

★   ★   ★

Through an aperture, I glimpse this world,
indifferent to my missing presence;

I witness its breezes render flags unfurled, though
I'm denied the simplest pleasance.

Impervious and secure, the fenestration
remains, allowing no entry or escape;

it isn't designed like other windowpanes, but
constricts sight with its miniscule shape.

A form of punishment is this meager view, taken
through glass, so scratched and fogged

are scenes that some can't bid adieu, no
matter how many days are logged.

Looking outside for anything new, like blades of grass or butterflies,

we regularly fail to take issue with reflections overlooked by our eyes.

Often, we ignore our mirrored visage and the possible metaphors therein;

our saddened gaze pleads for a mirage to distract us from the maudlin.

Despite how near the outside seems, that
freedom is just beyond our reach;

even after observing, aided by sunbeams, these
damned windows we cannot breach.

Yet, there is much more to behold than what we can see from within,

for such portals, though not solid gold, have a value with no margin.

From BOTH sides, things can be spied and insight can be gained

at openings dispersed far and wide, in placed unknown and famed.

Many similar gateways, though are merely allegories,

bringing to mind "Windows to the Soul",

where shy glances can tell entire stories

amid reflections that can make us whole.

BETWEEN THE LINES

★   ★   ★

Do you believe in the existence of fate, of your
whole life inscribed on some blessed slate?

Is your every movement steered by God's thumb, or
are you in control of your future's outcome?

In our path, I believe, certain people are placed
so we may know life and love interlaced;

but my behavior and choices are mine alone, not
predetermined by some deity, unknown.

None of us have a special destiny to fulfill because
we all possess the power of free will;

though many feel born to play a distinct role, no
Kismet abides to weigh upon their goal.

Our universe is too vast and chaotic for coincidence to
be the reasoning behind life's strange events,

yet happenstance is just an easy way to explain all
the odd incidents that our lives contain.

Regarding a creator, if one truly presides, never
actively interferes, but opportunity provides.

We decide for ourselves what our beliefs entail, and
between good and evil, which one will prevail.

However natural or divine a spectacle may appear,
don't assume it's origins are always crystal clear.

Many random mishaps are results of human design that
merely held some variable we failed to refine.

Nothing in all one's years is ever preordained, except
certainty of death, in our flesh ingrained;

for man's vagary disproves the notion of serendipity by
revealing life's correlations in all their simplicity.

WHAT COMPARISON?

★   ★   ★

I'm hard to kill and mad as hell, I'm lightning
quick with no need to yell;

you're a 'fraidy cat and a limp dishrag, you
shave your legs and dress in drag.

I chew on nails and spit out lead, I'm bulletproof, even on my head;

you eat Xanax and visibly shake, you avoid
all sincerity and promises, break.

I finish my jobs and keep my word, I take
out trash and won't be deterred;

you lie by default and betray your friends, you
piss sitting down and wear Depends.

I'm immune to toxins and never tire, I drink blood and breathe out fire;

you're overweight and love to trick, you glut on wieners and end up sick.

I excel in war and on offense, stand, I always
shoot first and scorch the land;

you beg for dope and act absurd, you pay for sex and cry afterward.

I have no limits and hone my senses, I blow
out walls and break down fences;

you're nearly deaf and a horrible shot, too, you
stutter all day and flinch on cue.

I know your traits and I ain't scared, I met
countless others and none were spared;

You think you're smart and sure to succeed,
you're already dead and a loser, indeed.

DREAMS

★   ★   ★

Dreams are sometimes different and sometimes just the same,

sometimes full of strangers, others, you know their names.

The things that you imagine in this midnight fantasy

will often haunt you when you wake and test your sanity.

You might dream of falling, or running very slow,

or hovering in air with nothing down below.

The visions that you have when you fall asleep

are the very ones that might give you the creeps.

Dreams might be scary and fill you up with fright

when you open up your eyes in the blackness of night.

It can be hard to fathom that dreams aren't reality

when they seem so real that it affects your mentality.

These mysteries that happen when you close your eyes

stay with you forever, even when you hide.

NIGHT SOUNDS

★   ★   ★

What to make of what I hear in the black of night?

I cannot tell from where it comes, if only there were light.

The noises strange and eerie, come from all around.

I fear I cannot move, my feet are frozen to the ground.

Are the sounds coming closer or is it only in my mind?

I'm scared to open up my eyes for fear of what I'll find.

The urge to flee is forceful but I'm uncertain where to go;

to run means that I am scared, fear I don't want to show.

Maybe if I cover my ears the noise will go away

and when I open up my eyes this will be another day.

With my ears still covered and my eyes closed tight

I wish for a miracle and pray with all my might.

The fear inside is mounting but I decide at last

to look around and listen, hoping this cadence has passed.

An then there was nothing but the rustle of the trees

and my waning terror floating on the breeze.

TIME

★   ★   ★

Today is the first day of the rest of your life,
amid the stress, worry and strife.

Past and present meld into one, then turn
to future when this day is done.

Another day, the same old way, and in this dreariness I must stay.

There is no end to this monotony; life goes on in a boring prophecy.

Every day, just like the last, except the times are changing fast.

Years goes by, yet here I am standing on these shifting sands.

Will these doldrums ever end? This is the message I'm trying to send.

In this tiring world, to remain here I must, until
the last moment when I turn to dust.

WHO I AM

★   ★   ★

Am I a predator or am I the prey? That depends on which tale you allay.

The one that names me as a stalker, who goes
on the prowl as it gets darker?

This is the story some choose to believe, that
I am a monster, I kill and I thieve.

I see no way to turn this around, as gossip
is rampant and rumors abound.

There is another side to me, a side that no one chooses to see.

They fail to accept the two sides of the coin,
and in the center is where they adjoin.

One transforms into the other with hardly a hint left to discover.

You cannot fathom both sides of me, that there
are two you'll soon come to see.

You'll hardly conceive of who I am and will
not believe till I show my hand.

And so I continue to live in this way as the
edges of the parts start to fray.

How long can I keep up this charade? Already too long I am afraid.

BEYOND MY REACH

★　　★　　★

Sometimes I want to be a child again, to relive those
days, but they've washed down the drain.

There is no way to go back in the past, to relive
the good times and make them last.

A teacher once told me to reach for a star but the
older I get makes it now seem too far.

There are so many, spread far and wide; to try
would be useless, so that delusion has died.

There've been days we've all reached for our dreams,
until our lives came apart at the seams.

They seemed so attainable in that place and time,
but over the years have become too sublime.

Memories are repressed in the back of my mind but
the fog of time makes them hard to find.

Try as I might, I fail to recall any of the thoughts or echoes at all.

I reach for the feelings deep down inside until
I realize they are trying to hide.

Buried and covered and hidden from me are
emotions that made me who I used to be.

I long to be able to come and go as I please, to
have the freedom to exit with ease.

The keys and the codes that keep me inside,
along with the rules, I must abide.

THE HOURGLASS

★   ★   ★

If I fall asleep to never awaken; the thought of
that leaves me trembling and shaken.

There are so many things I have yet to do, and
time is so short that I haven't a clue

where to start on my bucket list, so I clench my jaw and ball up my fists.

The years have slipped by without any notice and
now I don't even know where to focus.

I'm told I'm too old and I am too feeble to
travel or be around crowds of people.

My mind is not right and I cannot remember
if this is August or if it's September.

I don't want this to be the end of my days; in the
beginning there were so many ways

to try and fulfill all of my dreams, but time has run out, or so it seems.

I've waited too long to begin to live and there
are no days left for me to forgive.

There's no one to visit, nobody to care, I'm
left alone with my lingering prayer.

For God to rid me of this existence for I am
tired and have gone the distance.

I guess I'll just lay here in this bed and wait for
the moment I'm pronounced dead.

INFLICTION

★ ★ ★

Like a soldier's battle scars I proudly wear my pain;
it feels like a heavy ball attached to a chain.

It's with me every day when I open my eyes and
even when I'm sleeping it is waiting to arise.

The hurt took many forms, breaking trust and telling
lies, sexual perversion, and twisted alibis.

There is no way to quell it or hasten it to end and so
I've learned to cope and make it my friend.

I'm broken but beautiful inside and out but the pain
has made me who I am, of that I have no doubt.

It has taken many years to reach this conclusion
without ever a hint of mental confusion.

Somehow I've learned to use the pain to make me
strong so that now I can feel like I belong.

Dealing with the hurt that others have induced has
granted me serenity, even though I was misused.

I know I'm not alone in surviving this distress; others
have come before me and more yet to profess.

I hold no ill will and have no regrets, for those who've done me wrong will get theirs' in the end.

If I could start all over and live my life again I wouldn't change a thing, thanks for the pain.

INSIDE MYSELF

★ ★ ★

Don't believe or listen to the lies and rumors of who you are.

You know the truth and that's what matters, behind all the scars.

Everyone has their own story but this one's yours and yours alone.

You lived it but it doesn't have to control your future, your unknown.

Some people will never learn to accept their painful pasts

and embrace the hurt and sorrow, leaving bitterness that lasts.

Those who learn to love themselves despite their tears and fears

will have an inner peace that will stay throughout the years.

TELL ME WHERE TO LOOK

★ ★ ★

Is there a place to seek absolution? I hope it's easy to find.

Should I pursue forgiveness at church, or the back of my mind?

Maybe I'll find what I'm looking for walking along the coast.

Then again, it could be discovered in the places I go the most.

I could locate vindication beside a quiet trickling brook

or possibly in the letters whose meanings I mistook.

It seems the answers I'm looking for are just beyond my grasp

and hidden in some remote place, camouflaged and masked.

I don't know when I'll find it but I'll continue the quest

for until I find redemption my soul will not be at rest.

YOUR SPIRIT

★   ★   ★

It seems like you are right here with me watching my every move.

I feel your presence close to me but it's something I can't prove.

I often talk to you like you are sitting across the table from me.

You answer me back in the tiniest voice, and you it can only be.

No one accepts when I tell them you're here because they don't believe.

But I know it's you that's here and that thought gives me reprieve.

The feelings of assurance that you are close bring me comfort and peace.

No other sensations can even compare and I hope they will never cease.

BEFORE YOU SPEAK

★　　★　　★

Words can be like a double edged blade, they may
cut to the bone or make you unafraid.

Words may slice through your heart like a razor and
jolt your insides and your core like a taser.

Think a moment before you spit them out; you can't
take them back once you go that route.

Words can be used to hurt or to heal; the way
they're spoken can be hard as steel.

Feelings and emotions may get in the way and come
out of your mouth in the things you say.

You might not always understand their effect so
be careful in saying the words you select.

Words might be spoken to comfort or soothe,
and to your ear can sound very smooth.

Oral expressions can be misunderstood, and for
someone who's hurting, that is not good.

Always be mindful in the words that you say, just
a friendly reminder for you every day.

TRANSPARENT

★   ★   ★

I have faded into the background, lost in the great unknown.

I feel like nobody can see me; I'm lost in another time zone.

I surely must be invisible to people as they come and go;

they appear to look right through me as they walk to and fro.

Although I tread amongst them, never my shadow appears,

and though my footfalls are steady, it's as if no one hears.

I scream as loudly as I can, enough to wake the dead,

as I search for recognition, not one person turns their head.

Is this what it's like to be in limbo, not dead but not alive?

I'm yearning for the day when somewhere I will arrive.

LOVE SPELL

★   ★   ★

Love is a crazy emotion, like a runaway train.

There is no way to stop it or tell it to refrain.

It feels what it wants, you cannot hold it back,

as the runaway train is running off the track.

Love is rather crazy and can be unpredictable.

You never know when it will touch, it's contradictable.

It will sneak up on you like a ghost in the night,

and before you know it you are in the lovers light.

Love can strike in an instant, like a lightning bolt.

It may seem like you are shocked with electric volts.

It will make you tremble and stumble with your words,

and make your heart feel as if it's fluttering with birds.

It's hard to put in words and even harder to explain.

The loss of it can make a heart break with pain.

The love, if you can keep it, may fill one with pleasure

and carry through the years as life's greatest treasure.

ABOUT THE AUTHOR

Richard Sloane is the pseudonym of a career criminal well known to the state of Tennessee and it's justice system. A mere GED graduate with no journalism or related degrees, yet astoundingly knowledgeable and literate, Sloane has spent almost a quarter century exercising illicit skills while wrestling with abnormal motivations and a possible unhinged social disorder of the mind. From cat burglar, bodyguard, drug dealer and hired muscle, to nihilistic villain and radical hunter of sexual deviants and bullies, "Dickie" Sloane is the most experienced, driven and invisible outlaw you've never heard of. With no wife, children or any other real responsibilities forcing him to lay down roots, he has wandered in search of significance and satisfaction where few have dared to tread, and where fewer still have emerged ready for round 2.

Printed in the United States
By Bookmasters